Wild Wisdom
Listening from the Heart of Nature
WORKBOOK

OTHER BOOKS BY DAVID BRUCE LEONARD:

Medicine at Your Feet:
Healing Plants of the Hawaiian Kingdom

How to Worship the Goddess
and Keep Your Balls:
A Man's Guide to Sacred Sex

Wild Wisdom
Listening From the Heart of Nature
WORKBOOK

By
David Bruce Leonard

Illustrations by
M. Stone

Forward by
Kahu Dane Kaohelani Silva

Just what you need... another
Roast Duck Producktion

*"A peasant must stand a long time on a hillside with his
mouth open before a roast duck flies in."*
- - Chinese proverb

POD PRINTING VERSION ONE
July 2011

WORKBOOK
ISBN#   978-0-9800505-4-7
ISBN#   0-9800505-4-5

71 pages
16 illustrations
Softcover: 8in. x 10in.

cover & book design by Philip Brautigam
www.easy2yes.com

cover background painting by the remarkable Kit Gentry
www.kitgentry.com

Roast Duck Producktions
www.davidbruceleonard.com

david@davidbruceleonard.com

We have survived the past because
we have bent Nature to our Will.

We will survive the future
if we can bend our Will to Nature.

For my teachers.
They listened… and *heard*….

TABLE OF CONTENTS

ACKNOWLEDGMENTS

A Short List of Short-Duration-Personal-Saviors
Mitch Brinks
Steven Buhner
David Clausnitzer
James Duke
Steven Foster
Bob Hobdy
Kawika Ka'alakea
Kaipo Kaneakua
Bill Kanekoa
Ed and Puanani Lindsey
Dennis McKenna
Anna Palomino
Dale Pendell
Fred Stone
Rene Sylva
Tim Tunnison
Jill Wagner

I wish to thank those individuals who have contributed in some way to this work:
Philip Brautigam
Kit Gentry
Darrell Lapulapu
Jacob Leberman
Lobo
Sabrina Mata
Scott Rautman
Dane Kaohelani Silva
Sol Sebastian
M. Stone, Illustrator
Dale Strawhacker
Jack Weber

I especially grateful to Robert Newman who co-authored
a couple of sections in this book.
Thank you, Robert.

WARNING

Forward
by Kahu Dane Kaohelani Silva

As the late afternoon sun warmed his back and shoulders, the herbalist walked briskly across his garden, following a worn path between tall 'ōhi'a trees, bedecked with scarlet lehua flowers. Hearing a high-pitched humming sound from behind him, he turned quickly to identify the source of the vibration. Seeing no one behind him, he resumed his daily walk. Once more, the humming sound caught his attention, and he stopped and turned completely around to see what was making the vibration. At that moment, a ray of sunlight reflected off the yellow flowers of the low bush alongside the trail. Dropping to one knee, he examined the cluster of flowers and noted that their usual color had deepened to a beautiful, golden hue.

"Could this flower be the source of the humming sound," he wondered? Addressing the flowers directly with the thoughts in his mind, the herbalist asked, "What do you want?" He was surprised when he heard a response inside his head, "Use me!" "How do I use you", he asked. He felt the flowers smile and answer, "You will know when the time is right."

Heeding the request from the flowers, the herbalist offered a prayer of purification and blessing for the garden, and formally asked for permission from the plant to use it as a source of medicine. Stunned by the communication from the bush, the herbalist followed his formal protocol for gathering, storing and drying the plants under the shade of the deck at his small studio amongst the 'ōhi'a trees. A few weeks later, simply following his instincts as an herbalist, he prepared the flowers and leaves for heating in a large pot of olive oil. After soaking in the oil for an additional day, he separated the plant matter and poured the filtered oil into 500 ml containers that he stored in his refrigerator.

He did not know at that time how he was supposed to use the oil, but he was pleased by the delightful scent of the oil. Intuitively, he began to use it for self-massage on the areas of his body which suffered daily aches and pains from his work in developing his large garden. He noticed how rapidly those minor aggravations would dissipate after the application of the oil.

A couple of weeks later, the herbalist received a call from a friend of his who was in the hospital. The doctor had examined him and then told him that his lower right leg was gangrenous, and that he might need to amputate the blackened leg. The friend asked if there was anything that the herbalist could do to help him to save his leg. A feeling came over the herbalist that reminded him of the unusual communication that he had felt in the garden with the flowers. Could this be it? Is this what the plant medicine would heal?

The herbalist arrived at the home of his friend who had left the hospital, against his doctor's orders. If he had stayed in the hospital, he would have lost his leg, his friend told him. If he returned home, perhaps there was a chance of saving his leg, he reasoned. With the request for help from his friend as his guide, the herbalist instructed his friend to apply the oil to his own body, from the hip to the knee, from the knee to the foot, each day, for five days. He was advised to cover the leg with a clean cotton cloth each day, to protect it from external injury. After that, he was to stop using the oil for two days.

At the end of that period, the herbalist visited his friend again to observe the effects of the oil on the gangrenous leg. They spoke about the weather and family matters for a few minutes, putting themselves at ease. Finally, the herbalist asked his friend for permission to view his leg. Slowly, his friend unwrapped the right leg for inspection.

The natural brown color of the skin had returned over most of the front and side of the lower leg, with only a small border of darker skin around the sides and back of the leg. Healthier tissues at the surface of the skin had replaced the gangrenous tissue. Both friends were pleased with the initial results of the healing oil.

The herbalist advised his friend to continue to use the remainder of the oil as needed to restore the deeper tissues of the leg to health. They shared a prayer of thankfulness for the blessing that each of them had received as a result of this occasion.

Do you have an awareness of the plants in your garden or forest? Are they allies who support you on your path of healing yourself and others? Developing this awareness and openness can be facilitated by regular studies with an experienced herbalist, guide and instructor.

The author, David Bruce Leonard, is one of those gifted individuals who can translate the messages from the plants around us into the medicines and foods that can nourish our bodies, minds and souls. Blessed by the shared wisdom of traditional medicine from his teachers from across the globe, Kumu David openly shares those gifts with his students, patients and friends.

For more information about learning to interpret the gentle whispers from flowers and plants, consult expert healer and teacher, David Bruce Leonard. He can guide you to attain your own insights into the roles of plant allies on your personal path to the light.

EARTH - YIN
Living & Loving Between The Lines

EARTH - YIN
Living & Loving Between The Lines

Listening To The Earth - Listening To Each Other
I am at two with nature. ~ Woody Allen

We are profoundly disconnected from the Earth, from our bodies, from our unconscious "shadow", and from each other. Modern society has a long tradition of favoring scientific (reductionist) thinking over somatic (body-centered) awareness, and this has had a devastating effect on our quality of life. But science is the new kid on the block. Thousands of cultures throughout the millennia have cultivated a body-centered intelligence that is in line with the forces of nature and our environment. And they have done it without science.

Somatic awareness is not just some New Age concept; it is our natural state that has been smothered by hundreds of years and countless layers of cultural conditioning.

"Body-thinking" is our birthright ... it aligns us to our core, to our ancestors, and to the Earth itself. This is the part of us that falls in love or is moved by a sunrise. It is our body-knowing that expands our nostrils when we smell delicious food, or that knows when our partner is upset.

We don't have to imagine sprites or faeries in order to listen to the Earth. All we have to do is to reactivate the part of our nervous system that lies dormant and then pay attention.

Animals use this part of their nervous system all the time; they depend upon it for their survival. Dogs and cats use their body-knowledge to sense our mood and react accordingly. The wild animals that were our ancestors instinctively knew which plants to use as food and medicine. No one had to teach them.

The part of us that feels someone else's joy or grief is the same part that is outraged when a forest is clear-cut or when an oil tanker destroys a shoreline. Indeed, it is our disconnection from our own bodies that allows this to happen in the first place. Our disconnection from our bodies keeps us feeling powerless and small. When we feel our hairy warm-blooded nature and the miraculous beauty of the chemical messengers that surge in our blood, our path becomes clear and obvious. We have become refugees from our own biology.

This book is an introduction to reclaiming our birthright. This planet is our home and our Mother. We deserve to feel Her, our friends, and our loved ones in our spine, our nerves, and our flesh. We deserve to feel the Earth's pain and joy, and our Belovéd's pain and joy, in our belly. We deserve to come home to who we are.

Preparing The Ground Within Ourselves

In order to reactivate our nervous system and listen to the Earth, we must prepare the ground within us. That is, we must prepare our internal terrain to receive information. Much as we can help prepare soil to receive the plants of our garden, so can we prepare our inner "soil" to receive relevant information from the world and those around us.

There are many ways to do this... perhaps hundreds. And as different as they may seem from each other, many of these techniques are similar. Because human physiology is universal, different indigenous cultures have come to similar conclusions about how to optimize their nervous system and access a deeper knowing. Many of these practices involve presence, sensory awareness, and an embrace of seemingly extraneous information.

Like any other skill, our ability to listen deeply to the Earth and "live between the lines" can lie dormant with disuse or it can be enhanced through specific practices. These skills and practices for enhancing Earth-centered and body-centered intelligence were not extraneous cultural anomalies or curiosities. The survival of those people and their culture depended on the cultivation of these skills.

Getting Out Of The Way

We are conduits for the Earth and for the impulses of millions of years of evolution that preceded us. Each of us has within a physiological genius.

Our species survived for more than one hundred thousand of years by trusting our wild wisdom, the wisdom of our body. We relied on our somatic genius, and we did it without formal training in reading, writing, mathematics, or logic. Technology is fantastic, but it cannot replace one hundred thousand years of survival skills. We need not reject technology, but we must be aware of its limitations. We need to understand in what ways it should serve us, and in what ways it can never serve us.

In order to reconnect to the Earth we must find techniques that help us reclaim our biological inheritance. This has been accomplished by untold cultures in the past. What they discovered is that we can reclaim our somatic genius and prepare the ground for being conduits of the Earth is by *getting out of our own way*. We know much more than we think we know and are capable of much more than we believe. When we get out of our own way we give our idealized self a time-out. We suspend our disbelief and trust that suspension.

When we get out of the way, we engage the deepest parts of our nervous system, our biological inheritance. We surrender our judgments and we surrender to our intuition. We choose to put aside our cultural and psychological biases and limitations; we manifest the courage to make those biases conscious and transparent. We question everything we have been told, everything we think is real, everything we think may be possible or impossible.

While we question our intellectual and cultural assumptions, everything we do must be steeped in common sense. We must trust our intuition, the wisdom of our body and belly. While we are never 100% certain that we are correct, and we know that we do not need to be in order to make sane and intelligent choices.

When we get out of our own way we understand that we think too much with our head and not enough with our body. We cannot practice deep listening without getting out of our own way. And we cannot get out of our own way without first *learning to unlearn.*

Learning To Unlearn: Lessons From The Earth

The three most important qualities for learning to unlearn are: patience, humility, and respect.

Patience

Learning to listen deeply to plants, to the Earth, and to each other takes time. We have spent thousands of years moving away from our intuition, and now we are attempting to reclaim those parts of our nervous system that have "atrophied" from disuse.

Deep Listening is a learned skill, but we learn it by temporarily "removing" the layers of our "education" that smother us and prevent us from experiencing the world directly. In order to engage in Deep Listening, we will undoubtedly access parts of ourselves that are unfamiliar, and feel things part that we may not have felt since childhood. We may find ourselves way out of our comfort zone, deep into uncharted territory. This may test our patience. Navigating this unfamiliar terrain will test us, and our relationships.

We have spent a lifetime stifling our deep knowing; it is unlikely that we will reclaim it all within a year, or even within a lifetime. We will make mistakes... count on it. But, we can afford to be patient with ourselves, and those we love.

The Earth, and those we love, will reveal their mysteries to us in their own time. But they cannot share themselves any faster than our ability to hear them.

Humility

I may or may not know more than the person to whom I am listening. Or I may know more about some things but less about others. And just because I am human does not mean that I know more than a shrub does.... or a tree. I just may have something to learn.

Respect

In order for us to live, many things must die every day. If, in some deep and fundamental way we cannot experience plants as equal beings and honor the sacrifice we ask them to make, we will never be able to hear what they have to tell us.
It is also challenging to learn from someone or something we do not respect. When we learn how phenomenal plants really are, we understand that we actually have a lot to learn from them.

ROOTS
Reaching In - Listening to Ourselves

ROOTS
Reaching In - Listening to Ourselves
He 'A'ali'i ku makani mai au; 'a'ohe makani nana e kulä'ï.
I stand as strong in the wind as an 'A'ali'i tree; no gale can knock me down.
- - Traditional Hawaiian saying

INTRODUCTION TO ROOTING
Home Blindness: We Cannot See The Forest... Period.

In Sweden there is a concept called "home blindness". Home blindness is the term used for our inability to see the beauty of the place we live. We all succumb to home blindness eventually. It is, to a degree, part of our nature. Aldous Huxley referred to the brain as a "reducing valve", a device that limits the amount of information coming in so that it may focus on the task at hand without being overwhelmed. Creating familiarity with our surroundings is a way to reduce environmental distractions.

So while this may be a "natural" process, it still is something we must guard against. In some ways "home blindness" is the opposite of gratitude, and our gratitude for the natural world is one of the things that keeps us most connected to our source.

In a similar way, we can experience home blindness regarding those we love. Once the "bloom is off the rose", as they say, we can take the people we love for granted, sometimes treating them as the enemy.

In this also, rooting can help us.

Being Present - Lucid Waking

Many of us have had the experience of lucid dreaming, in which we are asleep and dreaming but we are simultaneously aware that we are dreaming. A lucid dream is a very powerful experience with vast potential.

Now how many times on any given day are we conscious that we are awake? When we are awake and aware that we are awake and aware, we are in a state of Lucid Waking.

Lucid Waking is the state of being fully present. When we are fully present in any given situation doors can open for us that might otherwise remain closed.

Lucid waking will often bring with it a natural curiosity as to what is happening both inside and outside of us. When Lucid Waking is combined with this natural curiosity, it becomes Deep Listening.

So, when we are practicing Deep Listening we are always curious and ready to learn what will happen next, or what will be discovered next.

EXERCISE: Lucid Waking

- If you want to, set a timer or alarm for 20-30 minutes
- Place yourself in a comfortable position, preferably sitting.
- Relax your body but keep your back straight... as if you were being pulled up toward heaven by the back of your head.
- Relax your jaw and let your hands sit comfortably on your lap. Yours eyes may be open or closed.
- Place your awareness on your breath, allowing yourself to breath fully and naturally.
- Continue to pay attention to your breathing. When you find your mind wandering, bring it back to your breath.

Reaching Inside & Listening to Ourselves

We have within us knowledge of who we are and what we need. This is our psychological core and our mammalian heritage. It is our birthright.

Many of us are conditioned from birth to ignore this part of ourselves, replacing it with the drive to please others. If we are not well grounded in who we are we become overly concerned with what we imagine other people are thinking about us.

Our drive to please others is evolution's way of keeping the tribe bonded together and assuring our ability to survive and reproduce. We are *hardwired* to care what others think of us, particularly other members of our peer group or tribe. There is nothing wrong with pleasing others, but when we do it at the expense of our core values, we betray ourselves in fundamental ways.

This pattern and conditioning is created at a very young age and can haunt us throughout our life if we do not address it.

Unfortunately, for many of us this is not a choice but an unconscious pattern that we perpetuate automatically without thinking.

If we are unsure of who we are, we can easily override our original voice the one that truly speaks our truth from our heart.

But we can reclaim our original voice, the voice that speaks from our core and knows what we want. In our reclamation it begins as a small faint voice but with diligence and practice we can learn to hear and speak that voice in our lives.

Shadow and patterns of the disowned self, when managed properly, are turned into fertilizer which in turn nourishes our roots. When we properly give our shit to the Earth, She rewards us with flowers.

We can develop the ability to validate our own perceptions of the world, to self-validate.

The solution to this is to reach in and listen to ourselves... to listen to that small faint voice within. Often that voice that as often as not communicates to us not through words but to sensations arising from our bodies, from deep within our nervous system.

The solution is to ground our spirit and to and root in our lives.

When we root in our lives, we root in them the way they really are, not as we might wish them to be. That space beneath us, that fertile Yin essence, is also our shadow.

Both Daoist and Hawaiian cultures practice a "dropping in" to the lower abdomen in order to navigate our world. This dropping in takes us to a place where we know who we are.

Dropping in is a somatic process, and whether we are conscious of it or not, we track it in our body. It can be slightly different for each of us, but the general movement of energy is the same; it runs from the head and neck down the torso and into the lower abdomen.

When we drop in, we listen to our deepest knowing. This is particularly useful when we are feeling "at effect" of other people's behavior or judgments.

Dropping in is also the means by which we use our body as an antenna.

If we can only receive nourishment from the outside world then we are unable to drink from our own well. Our rooting in our deepest sense of self is the means by which we receive nourishment from our own soil. This deep sense of self is also the ground in which we find our core values: the things in life that we value the most.

EXERCISE: Reaching Inside

- Think of a time when you made an agreement that you knew was not in your best interests.
- Try to recall when you first became aware of the self-betrayal. What were the red flags in the situation that you chose to ignore? What were the sensations in your body that let you know you had made a mistake? Try to isolate the quality and location of specific sensations.
- Stand up and shake your whole body vigorously and rub your face with your hands.
- Now recall a time when you were faced with a difficult or unpleasant task but somehow you "knew" you would be able to perform with confidence. Try to recall the sensations of confidence that let you know you were capable of accomplishing what you wanted to.
- When you have recreated the feeling of confidence in your body, create an "anchor" gesture to remind you of that sensation.
- Use that anchor gesture when you want to again access your core sense of knowing.

Differentiation

When we are rooted in our core self, we are in a state called differentiation, sometimes referred to as individuation.

When we are differentiated we understand and value the differences between another being and us. Without differentiation we are "at effect" of other people's opinions or external situations; those opinions or circumstances can sway us to such a degree that we betray the core of who we are.

When we are differentiated we recognize that to a significant extent we run our own nervous system. While we cannot always control what we are feeling we can influence how we react to those feelings and the choices we make around them.

Differentiation is a very important skill for generating self respect and respect for others. When we are differentiated we understand that other people, animals, and plants have their own valid perspectives. We can understand their perspectives without having their needs and perceptions unduly influence our own.

In cultivating wild wisdom, our differentiation is the uncovering of our core self. This is the part of ourself that is fundamental and non-negotiable.

EXERCISE: Differentiation

- Think of a time when someone said something hurtful to you and you felt wounded.
- Recall what they said and feel the emotional pain in your body. Where is the pain located?
- Bring your awareness inside and ask yourself "Did that person tell the truth? Is it true from my perspective and from my understanding of myself?" If you feel that the person who insulted you spoke the truth, would your best friend agree with you?
- For example, someone might have said to you, "You are ugly". You might have felt terrible. But when you look in the mirror, you may or may not agree with that assessment. Or you may say to yourself, "Well there are things about me that are not attractive, but there are many things I like about myself." Or "I was having a bad hair day, but normally I look pretty good!"
- This practice of comparing other peoples perceptions of us with our core values is what creates differentiation
- Stand up and shake your whole body vigorously and rub your face with your hands.
- Now recall a time in which someone tried to insult you but it had absolutely no effect. Try to recall the feeling in your body when you realized that the "insult" had not landed anywhere on you. What were the differences between the two situations? Often, for an emotional wound to land on us we are often somehow complicit. Did some part of you secretly agree with the first person but not with the second?

Rooting

Rooting is the physiological sensation of dropping into our core values and core identity. Rooting combines aspects of lucid waking, internal locus, reaching inside ourselves, and differentiation.

We root to come home to the Earth and ourselves. We need to root in our love and family relationships. We need to root to listen to a plant, to make difficult choices, and to determine our core values.

The Earth holds our deep shadows, our core values, and our integrity. For most of us, to discern our core sense of self and our core values we must embody integrity, i.e., we must be integrated within ourselves. When we are conditioned as children to ignore our core self we become, by definition, *dis-integrated* ("out of integrity").

Of course, none of us is completely integrated. We all have shadow that we must work through to turn into fertilizer. But the more integrity we can manage to generate in our lives and the more our behavior is aligned with our deepest values, the more nutrition our roots can derive from our soil.

When we root, we come down out of our head and we move our internal locus into our lower abdomen, or down our legs into the Earth.

EXERCISE: Rooting

• Rooting is challenging to describe. Although it involves many aspects of the techniques mentioned above, it is primarily a somatic process, a process we feel in our body.
• Come into lucid waking, the present moment, and bring your internal locus into your head. Get a sense for what that feels like in your body.
• Now quickly drop your internal locus into your lower abdomen.
• Make note of any differences between the two loci

PHYSIOLOGY OF ROOTING
Reclaiming the Yin and Yang of Our Nervous System

We have two basic divisions within in our autonomic nervous system: The sympathetic nervous system and the parasympathetic nervous system.

The sympathetic nervous system is often referred to as "fight, flight, or freeze". This part of the nervous system is mediated by the chemical adrenaline. When we experience fear, fright, anger, or strong emotional reactions, adrenaline is released into our bloodstream. We then will fight, run away, or freeze in response.

The parasympathetic nervous system is sometimes called "rest and digest", or "feed and fornicate". This part of the nervous system is mediated by acetylcholine. When we are more relaxed and "centered", and there is no imminent physical or psychological threat, acetylcholine is released into the blood stream, putting us into a "rest and digest" mode, or sometimes into a state of romantic arousal.

The sympathetic and parasympathetic nervous systems complement, and ideally, work together, much like the accelerator and brakes on a car.

Because of our pace of life in modern society, we spend an unnecessary amount of time in a sympathetic high adrenaline state of fight or flight. We commonly call this being "stressed out".

The Chinese refer to this state of high stress as "time disease", a state in which we do not give ourselves enough time to get things done. There are many causes and sources of time disease in our lives. The corporate media that bombards our senses with ever increasing rates of stimulation generates some of this. But we also give ourselves time disease by scheduling too much in one day. Situations arise and we fail to factor in our quality of life while planning our time. "Wow, I have an extra ten minutes I think I'll wash my car!" Later we find ourselves thinking "Why am I always late?" Or we become addicted to the drama of constant stimulation around us. We often mistake stress for excitement and fail to grasp the crisis mentality that permeates our lives.

This chronic state of high adrenaline is particularly damaging to us. In stressful states more than adrenaline is released into our body. Cortisol is another chemical that the body releases during stressful states that keeps us from dying of shock. But the same cortisol levels that keep us alive in the short term may also make us prone to autoimmune disorders, heart attack, or stroke if elevated blood levels continue for extended periods of time

Stress severely impacts our ability to connect with our world, and to connect with each other. We cannot digest our food well, listen deeply to a loved one, or access our deep listening skills when we are in a high-adrenaline stressed-out state of being. So if we are to reconnect with the Earth and those we love, we must be willing to step off of the hamster wheel long enough to catch our breath.

Fortunately, we have the ability to consciously choose to make a shift from a stressful state to a non-stressful one. When we make this choice we simultaneously change our physiology: Our heart rate, blood pressure, and levels of cortisol in the body all drop. In this comfortable parasympathetic state we have the opportunity to become physically relaxed and emotionally content.

Brain Mind, Heart Mind, & Belly Mind

In developing wild wisdom and deep listening skills, we must learn to use specific parts of our body in different ways. Many traditions distinguish three centers of thought or emotion, the head, the heart, and the gut. Each of these serves a different function for us as we relate to the world.

Brain Mind - Po'o

We think from our head. Not a bad idea, if you think about it. If we are going to think at all, the head is the optimum place from which to do it. Lots of great neurons up there, grey matter galore, and enough synapses to fill a universe of possibilities... all in a softball-sized wad of Jello crammed into a tightly packed cranium.

Symbolically speaking, the head is our linear mind, the seat of logic and linear thinking. We need it to conceptualize and communicate ideas, to do things like math and engineering, and to understand logic and science.

But alas in many ways we live in a non-linear universe, and our brain mind does not always serve our humanity as a reliable tool. My Hawaiian teachers always said that the head would fool you, but that the na'au, or intuitive belly would never betray you. They correctly observed that the lower belly to be an accurate place from which to navigate in the world; that it reveals a more reasonable representation of what is happening around us.

In traditional cultures there is often a focus on bringing awareness down from the head and into the torso and abdomen.

This sometimes is directed to the chest, but more often the awareness is moved lower into the belly.

A portion of the parasympathetic nervous system is mediated by the tenth cranial nerve, also known as the vagus nerve. The vagus nerve emerges from the brain stem and connects with the larynx, the heart, the digestion, and parts of the reproductive organs, spreading throughout the lower abdomen.

Heart Mind - Pu'uwai

We speak from our heart. Yep, not from the larynx... from the heart. Do you know how people say "He's all heart", or "She has a heart as big as the sky". We understand intuitively what they mean. Someone who speaks from the heart is often the kind of person who lives transparently and without shame. They usually reveal themselves without apology or arrogance.

In some traditions the upper torso (solar plexus or heart center) is the region from which we *speak* our clearest and most profound truths. Speaking from our heart is different than speaking from our head. Speaking from the heart involves an internal commitment to hearing ones own visceral and somatic responses and validating them, and communicating them clearly but without malice. These responses can be commented upon by the thinking mind, but never trumped by it, at least not in matters of consequence.

Belly Mind - Na'au

When we say that we know something "in our guts", or that "deep down we knew what was happening" what does it mean?.

It means that we have the ability to listen from our belly.

Many traditional practices present this accessing of one's deeper self and intuition as a somatic process. People in traditional cultures understood that the best way to reconnect with nature, the universe, and each other is *through the center of our body*, through the "root" of our awareness. Because the information we gather in such a state is unfiltered through our layers of conditioning, it can be a more direct way of knowing.

In a practical sense what this means is that we must access the world through a different part of our nervous system than the one we normally use. To experience deep listening we must go back in time to experience the world in a way that is pre-intellectual … a world we experience through our skin, through our organs, through our viscera.

Our pre-intellectual heritage involved using our instincts, our somatic perceptions, to guide our behavior. This is a visceral, non-cognitive process. Our heart-mind and our belly-mind are what remain of our deep inherited instincts. We use them as much as possible when we are involved in deep listening. We can use our belly mind when we are listening to the forest, a stone, a thunderstorm, or a loved-one.

Many traditional societies have a specific term for the lower abdomen. In China it is called the "dan tian" and in Japan the "hara". My Hawaiian teachers referred to this area in the lower abdomen as "na'au".

In Chinese, the term dan tian means "elixir field". The character dan implies a precious medicinal substance and also an alchemist's furnace. So this elixir field is a place in which powerful realizations and transformations can occur. Interestingly, this area is also called "ming men" which means "gate of destiny", implying that through accessing this part of our body we might align ourselves with our true nature and calling.

In Japanese, the word hara means "field". In the Japanese meditation practice of zazen, the fingers and thumb are formed into a circle in front of the hara. This practice brings one's attention and awareness to the lower abdomen.

In Hawaiian, the word na'au means the guts, the viscera or intestines, specifically referring to the lower abdomen and the area around the navel. But the word na'au also has a deeper meaning; it means knowledge. One perceives or knows ('ike) with one's na'au, but it is an unusual kind of "knowledge", a deeper and somatic knowledge rather than an intellectual one.

There is another Hawaiian word: "ao". The word ao refers to light as in daylight, but also to a spiritual light. So if we take the word na'au and we add the word ao (i.e., we shed "light" on our "knowledge") we get the word na'auao, which is the Hawaiian word for wisdom or enlightenment. This implies that if we bring self-awareness to our na'au over time we might shed light upon our knowledge we may access our wisdom, or even enlightenment. We access our na'au while in the forest in order to active those long-dormant parts of our nervous system, to see, feel, and express in ways that reflect who we are at our core, without all our cultural and intellectual overlays.

EXERCISE: Thinking Mind & Feeling Mind

• Go into the yard or the woods and select a plant that you are attracted to or seems to be "calling" you. Ask a plant permission to gather a piece of it.

• Examine the plant carefully. See how many different visual details you can notice. This would include things such as the number of hairs, color differences between one part and another, the number of veins per leaf, the shape of the leaves and if they are toothed, or any differences between one part of the plant and another.

• Stand up and shake your whole body vigorously and rub your face with your hands.

• Pick up the plant again and see how the plant makes you *feel*. Pay attention to what happens in your body as you see, touch, and smell it.

Deep Listening And Our Nervous System

He ala ehu aku kënä.
That is a misty path.
- - Hawaiian saying

Massage, yoga, and meditating can all shift us from a sympathetic to parasympathetic state. There are also little known "short cut" techniques that can quickly facilitate a change in our nervous system. Some of these techniques involve specific use of the eye muscles and positioning of the jaw. Others involve focusing one's attention on the lower abdomen.

As mammals we are born with this intuitive part of our nervous system. This "gut knowing" is our birthright. For many of us living in Western society, the ability to access this part of our nervous system has diminished through disuse; it has become dormant. People living closer to the land have relied on this part of their nervous system for millennia. It connects them to Nature and allows them to see Her the patterns and fluctuations.

This "gut knowing" is the place from which we perceive distress in the body of a loved one. It is also the reason that our house pets can seem to "read" our mood or intention.

For us as humans, bringing our awareness to our na'au and using specific neurological techniques to quiet our mind can help us open to this non-linear awareness. And while these techniques are simple, they may not be easy. It can take a lot of practice to become "fluent" in this "body-centered language".

Bringing our awareness to that part of our body may help us access our "rest and digest" consciousness. I believe this practice can also help us facilitate what we call intuition, or (literally) "knowing something in our guts".

This "knowing from the gut" is a body-centered state of awareness. While it can be accessed from a high adrenaline state it is much easier to do so from a more relaxed and "untriggered" parasympathetic state.

Intuitive awareness may help us to perceive our environment directly without impediment from our cultural biases and psychological filters. What can look like "magic" to an outsider is really just the activation of the "unused" parts of our nervous system. Animals use this "intuition" all the time, both in their dynamics with other creatures and in choosing what to eat. Monkeys, chimps, elephants, dogs, and cats have all been shown to use specific plants as "medicines". How do they know what to eat and what to avoid? I suspect that they use the same " body-centered awareness" that we can activate in ourselves.

Many traditional practices take advantage of this relaxed state; what is sometimes called "attention without tension". The Hawaiian practice of using non-linear awareness to gather and listen to plants is called hakalau, sometimes translated as "the breath of the leaf". Hakalau uses peripheral vision and the awareness of the lower abdomen to facilitate a shift into an altered neurological state that is deeply rooted in the parasympathetic nervous system.

We can use traditional modalities such as acupuncture, massage, and plant medicine to help us relax and increase our quality of life. Acupuncture points such as *fengchi* (GB 20), *wanggu* (SJ 14), *yintang*, and *baihui* (DU 20) can also help to induce a deeply relaxing parasympathetic state, as can Chinese or Hawaiian herbs.

And of course, we are not in this alone; we need to reconnect with those around us. With the help of others, we can make our lives, and our planet, suitable for human habitation.

ROOTING AS HEALING
Shamanism

Earth-based intelligence is inherently shamanic. Even if we are not "healers" or health care providers, our lives are steeped in tribal and shamanic practices.

If we read an astrology column, take an aspirin, prepare a cup of mint tea for a tummy ache, or comfort a friend who has the blues, we are functioning in a shamanic realm.

Our 300,000-year old hunter-gatherer tribal heritage has infused within us an innate drive toward using another member of our "tribe" to facilitate our healing process. Tribes naturally create, and gravitate toward, their shamans, the facilitators of their healing.

Like indigenous cultures, indigenous medicines and their progenitor shamanic systems emerged from the interactions between spirit, people and the land. All indigenous healing systems share common ground.

1) There is the laying on of hands.
2) There is prayer, divination, and mystical journeying.
3) There is plant medicine.
4) Attention goes to the natural world for validation.

When we engage in any healing practice we function as a shaman whether we are conscious of it or not. From an unconscious and archetypal level, a physician, chiropractor, or acupuncturist are all indistinguishable from a shaman. For the practitioner and the patient an archetypal relationship is hardwired into their DNA.

The archetype in the West is that of Chiron, the Wounded Healer. Chiron is a shaman. So is the Surgeon General.

That stethoscope around the neck of the physician is a rattle. Her diagnosis is divination. Her archetypal function makes her an intermediary or link between the patient and the Dao (health, wholeness, integrity, and unity).

When she "diagnoses" she is on a mystical journey, gathering information from the realm of the "Gods" and returning to the patient to translate indecipherable runes and words into practical information. It does not matter if her diagnosis comes from experiences in an ayahuasca journey or from a medical journal. It makes no difference if the indecipherable message she brings back are the words "interstitial cystitis" or a chant to the Jaguar God; the unconscious relationship between practitioner and patient remains the same. She interfaces between the patient and mysterious realm of the infinite using her skills of diagnosis (*literally*: "via knowledge").

> **Dao (Universe/Integrity)**
>
> **D**
> **I**
> **A**
> **G**
> **N**
> **O**
> **S**
> **I**
> **S**
>
> **dia (through) gnosis
> (knowledge)
> Practitioner (Shaman)
> Rx = Radix
> Hä = Breath**
>
> **R   B   T
> O   R   O
> O   E   U
> T   A   C
> S   T   H
>   H**
>
> **Patient**

This primordial relationship is part of our heritage and built into our species. We cannot ignore its significance or impact on our lives.

We are all capable of functioning in a shamanic realm and, indeed, we do so every day without being aware of it. Watching a sunset, making love, even falling asleep can bring us to a shamanic state. This is a very natural state four our nervous system, but because we are not accustomed to focusing or encouraging it, the state passes by quite unnoticed.

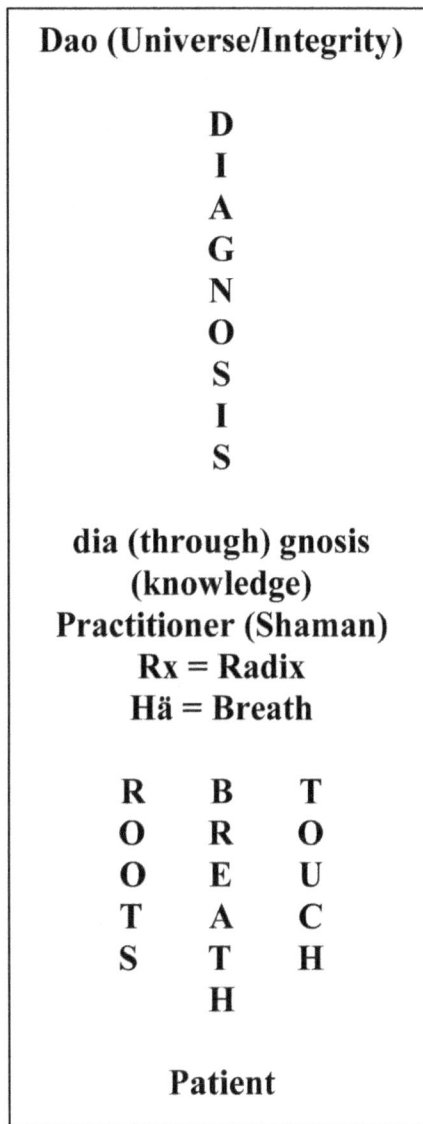

To live our lives well we need to use all the resources at our disposal, including all the rusty unused parts of our nervous system.

Medicine must be more than lab tests and injections.

Both the neurosurgeon and the medical intuitive are missing important pieces of the puzzle. It makes no more sense to treat a patient using only one half of your brain than it makes sense to run a race using only one of your legs.

To limit ourselves to science when making choices cheats us out of the fullness of our possibilities.

TRUNK
Clearing the Vessel

TRUNK
Clearing the Vessel

OPENING THE CHANNELS
Stillpoint

To cultivate an Earth-based intelligence we must take responsibility for how we navigate our own nervous systems.

We have very little control over the scripting that is created in us when we are infants and children; but these scripts continue to run in us until we die. Yet, while we had minimal control over our scripting, our part in their perpetuation is enormous. Our scripts may control our feelings to a large degree, We cannot always control our feelings, but we are always responsible for our behavior and how we react to those feelings.

When we are triggered, either because of the potential for physical danger or from emotional distress, our nervous system moves into a high adrenaline state. We can experience this when we are suddenly frightened or when someone insults us.

A high adrenaline response is a reasonable way to respond to being chased by a hungry lion, but it is not as useful when navigating a crying infant or an angry spouse.

There are numerous ways in which we can calm down from a high adrenaline sympathetic response. We can self-soothe by beating a pillow, taking pharmaceutical drugs such as valium, exercise, or use one of many neurological tools to help us regain equilibriumOne good way to shift from a high adrenaline sympathetic response to state to a more relaxed and effective parasympathetic response is with a technique I call Stillpoint.

EXERCISE: Stillpoint

To experience Stillpoint, flatten the curve on the back of your neck bringing the chin toward the neck and lengthening the spine. The feeling is as if the back of your head was pulling you up toward heaven.

Relax the shoulders.

Close your eyes. Relaxing the eyes is a critical part of experiencing Stillpoint. While Stillpoint can be done with the eyes open, it is best to learn it with the eyes closed. Bring your awareness to the back of your eye sockets and relax your eyes. If you like you can look at the back of your eyelids, but be sure to keep your eyes relaxed. Check the front, back top and sides of your eyes to see if there is any residual tension in any direction. Take note of the distinct sensation of having your eyes and eye sockets completely relaxed.

Now relax your neck and jaw completely leaving your mouth slightly open. Let your jaw float in a state of weightlessness. Relax the soft palate at the back of the roof of your mouth. Take note of the distinct sensation of having your neck and jaw completely relaxed.

Move your attention back and forth between the relaxation in your eyes and the relaxation at the back of your jaw. Try to connect the sensation of relaxation between the two areas.

As a more advanced technique, you can increase the power of Stillpoint by doing the following. With your eyes and jaw relaxed imagine that you are *looking at the back of your own eyes from the back of your head*. In other words, it is as if you have *another* set of eyes at the back of your head through which you are looking at the back of your eyes.

Doing this exercise for as little as 3-4 minutes can shift your physiological and psychological state from anxiety to relaxation.

Allow yourself to move into Stillpoint without falling asleep. Doing it while sitting in a chair will help.

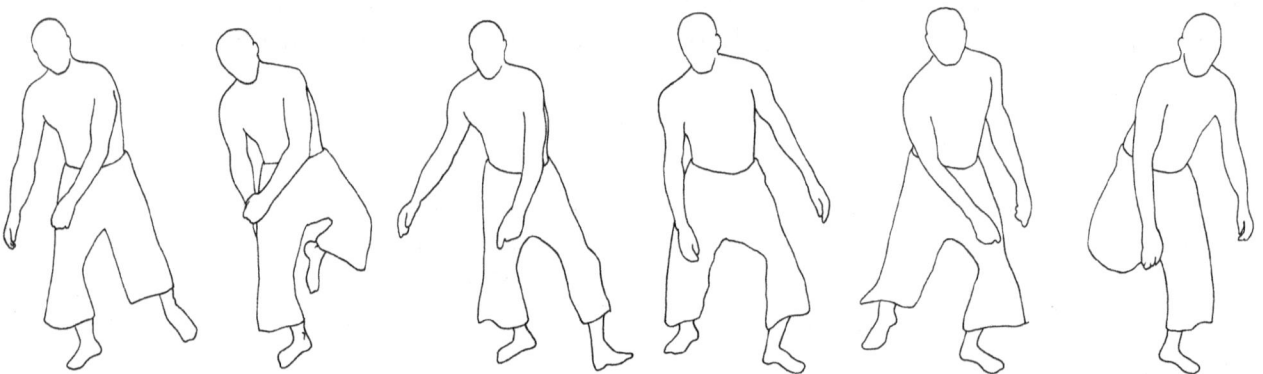

A Rooted Gait: Walking like a Primate

Because we spend so much time in our thinking mind, much of our energetic life force moves up in our body. This works well while calculating mathematics but is much less effective for listening to the forest.

When we are gathering plants and find ourselves too much in our head, we can use a "rooted gait" to bring awareness back down into the Earth.

EXERCISE: Rooted Gait

• Find an open flat area where you can walk.

• Wear comfortable clothing and good shoes if you need them.

• Begin to walk as if you were a non-human primate, a chimpanzee or a gorilla.

• Allow your arms and hips to swing naturally and keep your knees as bent as is comfortable. You want to feel the weight of your body upon your legs and the Earth.

• Feel your center of gravity sway with each step and the way your upper body and lower body movements compensate for each other.

• If you want to, you can combine the Rooted Gait with the Dermis exercise or the Hakahele practice described later in this book.

Praying with Our Bodies: Gathering Posture

Posture and physical alignment is important when gathering plants, walking in the woods, doing Qigong, or learning Deep Listening. A strong energetic posture aligns the structure and energetic "flow" of our body with the task at hand. In a strong posture our spine is straight with both lumbar and cervical curves flattened. To straighten the lumbar curve, tuck the pelvis under the torso. To straighten the cervical curve, lift the back of the top of the head pointed toward heaven.

Of course, gathering plants from the forest often means falling on our bottoms, scrambling over rocks and fallen trees, and generally moving in a non-impressive way. If we are getting scratched and bruised while looking to spend time with our plant friends this is a good sign. We are extending ourselves to meet our friends; this is just part of the process of being in the forest. We do not need to look cool; we need to connect with what is around us in a significant way. Still, when we can, it is good to adopt a posture and breathing pattern that enhances our experience and attentiveness.

Keep your hands empty while moving in a gathering gait. The shoulders are relaxed and forward with the arms swinging freely in order for you to be rooted in the process.

The knees are bent and the legs act like shock absorbers springs as we move allowing the torso to flow evenly under uneven terrain. When moving up riverbeds keep your steps short and sure-footed. The center of gravity is kept as low as can be comfortably managed.

The feet should be comfortable and if the terrain is difficult, the ankles should be well supported.

CLEARING THE CHANNELS
Aligning The Conduit: Clearing Trauma From Our Body

We all have the effects of physical and emotional trauma in our tissues and nervous system. While our body's initial reason for storing trauma in is to assure our physical survival, the residual effects of trauma unfortunately can seriously impede our quality of life. The residual effects of this trauma impede our ability to feel Because the physical and emotional effects of trauma can accumulate over time,

Physical and emotional trauma can also prevent us from changing our behaviors, even if that change might significantly increase our quality of life.

Locating Our Grief, Uncovering our Fear

Physical and emotional trauma is frozen within our nervous system when we are in a high-adrenaline state. It makes sense that we might somehow release that trauma through high adrenaline role-playing and emotional facilitation. This seems to be the case.

Because of the sensitive nature of this work is best done in a controlled setting with a licensed or well-trained facilitator.

Tribes in traditional cultures have long used similar practices to keep their members physically and psychologically healthy. Native American tribes have been known to engage in extreme physical and emotional tests and rites of passage. In Africa, there are traditional grieving rituals for men that facilitate their physical, emotional and spiritual awakening.

These practices helps tribal members transform previous psychological trauma while simultaneously giving them safety and license to open the energy channels of their body and attune themselves to all sorts of physical and psychological sensations.

In the West we now have similar initiations and rites of passage that serve the same purpose. Some of us are taking part in the current revival of traditional practices like sweat lodges and the Sun Dance. We are also recreating and adapting these practices unique ways that serve our social and psychological needs.

Rites of passage and emotional facilitation allow us to navigate our spiritual and psychological pain in a way that helps us access the deeper context of our lives.

When this vessel, our body, is not as cleared as we might like we can become cut off from our source and the rooting we have in our lives. Cut off from our core, we can become miserable, stifled and dysfunctional. We feel we have no place to stand in our own lives.

Our emotional health has a profound impact on our quality of life, physical vitality, and our ability to receive physical and psychological nutrition. When our pain is suffocated and trapped within our muscle memory it can cause physical and energetic stagnation. Eventually this pain can fester leading us to become abusive, self-destructive or passive-aggressive. When we clear trauma from our body we get psychological and spiritual air that can help to keep us from repeating our patterns.

This stagnation can impact our physical as well as our spiritual health. With continued low-grade muscle tension the blood and lymph supply of our tissues is compromised. Chronic low oxygen and inadequate lymph drainage can increase inflammation, reduce organ function, and increase the build-up of toxins. Men whose chests are immobile with body armor and cannot feel their own feelings can develop asthma or heart disease. Women who have shut down sensation in their pelvis can develop numerous physiological imbalances such as interstitial cystitis or ovarian cysts.

BRANCHES
Reaching Out - Listening to Nature

BRANCHES
Reaching Out - Listening to Nature
EXTENDING BRANCHES TO GAIA
Kapu (Sacred) Space

A Kapu Space is a place deep inside of ourselves that nothing can touch. It is a psychological and neurological sanctuary from which we visualize outcomes and access deeper parts of ourselves.

One of the things we can do before we embark on a journey to gather medicines or explore an area is to have everyone involved drop into a Kapu Space and visualize a happy, safe, and prosperous outcome. This usually involves visualizing everyone returning safe and happy when the group comes back from its journey. Visualizing from a Kapu Space, especially group visualization, magnetizes the unconscious minds of members group and gives them an orientation and an outcome to align with.

Sometimes a Kapu Space is created alone, however. This is particularly true when we listen to plants.

Qigong with Plants

Qigong originated in ancient China and became a favorite pastime of the Daoist and Buddhist monks. Legend has it that the man who brought Buddhism from India to China also brought exercises that later became the precursors to Qigong.

The word "Qigong" means *working with Qi*, or *working with energy*. As the Chinese word Qi means *air* as well as energy, Qigong can also mean *working with air* or *working with the breath*. There are thousands of Qigong exercises, each based on the building, movement, or draining of Qi.

Almost any qigong practice that we do alone we can do with plants. Plants have a very clear and powerful presence if we are only willing to be quiet enough to hear what they have to say.

Plants lend themselves well to sweeping Qigong movements and breathing exercises, but there are many

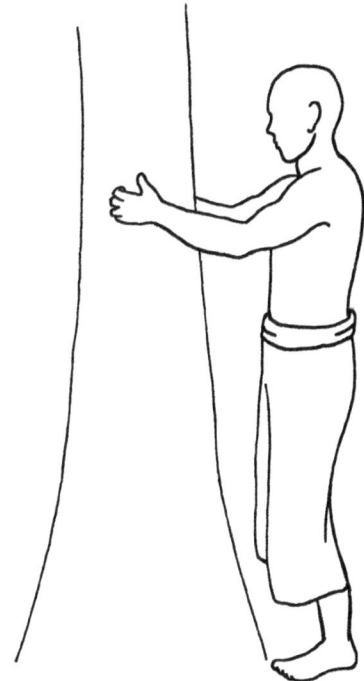

Qigong with a tree

ways to exchange energy with plants. The simplest way to connect with a plant is to just hold your hands near it and pay attention to what you are feeling. We will discuss this later on in this book.

On a fundamental level our relationship with plants is completely symbiotic: We use their oxygen and they use our carbon dioxide. This relationship is somewhat ironic, as when we really look at our relationship with plants, we cannot live without them, but they would do just fine without us.

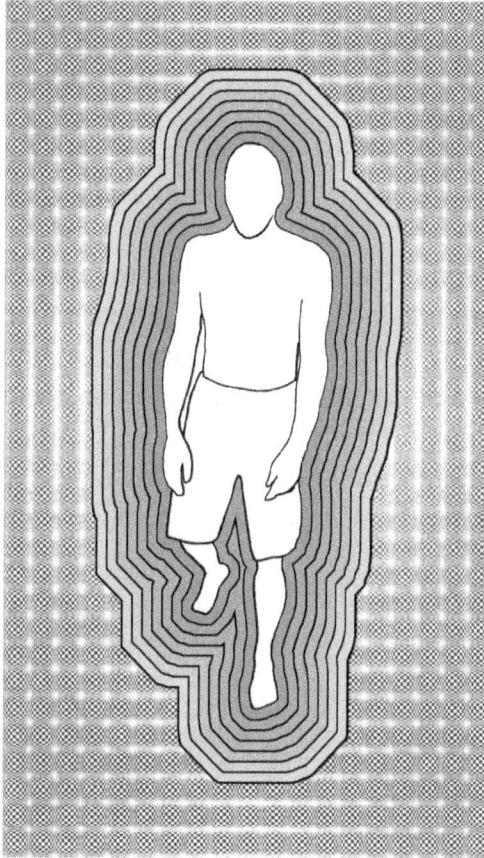

Body As Antenna /
The Skin is the Eyes of Our Core /
Seeing with the Skin

One of the ways we can learn to really experience plant gathering or even just walking in the woods is to practice "seeing" the forest through our skin. The simplest way to begin is to notice the sensations on your skin as you walk through a forest. You will feel breeze, your clothing against your skin, perhaps branches and leaves touching you as you walk, and sensations of warm or cool as your skin is touched by sunlight or shade. As you develop and refine this sense you will be able to feel the heat of people's bodies as the pass you on the trail or the sidewalk. The more you pay attention to these sensations, the more you will realize how much information our bodies process without our conscious awareness.

EXERCISE: Dermis Practice
- Find a place in nature where you can walk through the woods or in a park with a lot of different types of terrain and plant life.
- Center yourself and take note of what you are feeling on your skin. Walk slowly, noticing how the feelings in your body (and possibly emotions) change as you move through certain areas. These feelings are often very distinct yet not easily described in words.
- Move in and out of sunlight and shadow.
- Pay particular attention to sensations of temperature and touch. Note the way your skin feels on your clothing, the wind feels on your back. Pay attention to humidity and dryness. the warmth of sunlight and the coolness of shade.

- As you move through different areas and terrains pay attention to emotions and other sensations that might be triggered by these stimuli.

EXERCISE: Advanced Dermis Practice

- Find a place in nature where you can walk through the woods or in a park but where there are other people walking on the same path.
- As there are people walking past you on the trail, see if you can notice the heat from their bodies as they pass by you.

FOCUS AND LOCUS
The Eyes Have It: Soft Focus

In this book I frequently use the term "soft focus" to describe a technique that is done with the eyes. When we soft focus on something, our eyes are focused upon it but we are not necessarily concentrating on what we are looking at. Or, put another way, we are focusing on something but our eyes are as relaxed as they can be without losing visual focus.

The following exercises are all connected to the eyes. In the Chinese, Native American, Yogic, and Hawaiian cultures the eyes are used in very similar ways to create sensitivity and increase the depth of perception. Native American cultures called their eye techniques Owl Eyes. Hawaiian eye practices are called Hakalau. I have found these techniques immensely useful in helping me connect with the natural world.

While much of what I am addressing here is speculation, I believe that further advances in neurological science will verify that the way we use our eyes directly impacts our nervous system and the way it serves us.

EXERCISE: Soft Focus

- Select something to look that is right in front of you and rest your gaze on it.
- Lengthen your spine and take a deep breath.
- Relax your jaw and your face.
- Relax the muscles around your eyes and allow yourself to move into Stillpoint.

EXERCISE: Distal Soft Focus

- Select something far away from you and rest your gaze on it.
- Lengthen your spine and take a deep breath.
- Relax your jaw and your face.
- Relax the muscles around your eyes and allow yourself to move into Stillpoint.

Our Internal Locus

The Qi follows the thinking. - - Traditional Chinese medical saying

If you had to point to one part of your body that holds the center of your consciousness which part would you identify? I call this self-identified center our "internal locus".

Our "internal locus" is the place in our body that draws our attention and with which we most identify as "ourselves". Some of this will depend on where we are currently focusing our attention, but it also is determined by the body location to which we habitually default as our identity.

The location of our internal locus is subjective and appears to be different in different cultures. In numerous traditional cultures the internal locus is most often identified as the chest or abdomen. In the West, most of us identify most strongly with our head. In other words the part of our body that houses our consciousness is our head; we believe that the place in our body where we "*really*" live is in our head.

If we think our locus is in our head, where exactly in our head is it? Is it directly behind the eyes? Lower or higher? More to the front or the back?

Does our internal locus have a size? Is it as big as a melon? A grape? The head of a pin? Does the size and location stay the same or does it change depending on our state of mind?

Because our internal locus is subjective and self-identified, we have control over its size and location to a certain degree. We can consciously shift its location with a little practice.

The Chinese have a saying "The Qi (energy) follows the thinking." What this means is that when we think of a specific place in our body, the energy of our body goes to that place. By shifting our internal locus, we can change the kinds of signals we receive and the things we notice about ourselves.

When Chinese and Western men are asked to think of themselves during a brain scan a certain part of their brain is activated, the same part of the brain for both groups of men. And when Chinese men think of their mothers, the same part of the brain becomes active as when the think of themselves. But when Western men think of their mothers, a *different* part of the brain is activated.

So culture can strongly affect the way we use our brains and our nervous system. And perhaps, through changing our internal locus, we also might alter the physiology of our nervous system, including the way we gather and process information about the world around us.

EXERCISE: Internal Locus Practice

- Sit or stand comfortably with your eyes closed.
- Notice as thoughts arise in your mind. Pay attention to how your body reacts as the thoughts appear.
- Where do the reactions to your thoughts appear in your body? Are they in the same place or somewhere different each time?
- After you notice the reactions of your body to your thoughts, is there any place in your body to which your attention returns?
- Now open your eyes. Look around your environment keeping your awareness in your head.
- Once you have done this, begin to bring your awareness lower, into your neck. Scan your environment from the perspective of your neck. Has your perspective changed? If so, how do things "look" and "feel" from the perspective your neck?
- Do the same thing, scan the room, but this time try identifying more with the front or back part of your neck as you scan. Is there any difference between the two perceptions?
- Do the same thing with your chest, abdomen, arms, and legs. Take note of any subtle shifts in your awareness as you do so.

Our External Locus & Peripheral Attention

When we are paying attention to something outside of our body, I refer to the object of our attention as our "external locus".

Our external locus *may or may not be where our eyes are focused*; it is determined by where our attention is placed.

For example, in Qigong or Hakalau eye practices described in this book, our eyes are "focused" on something in the distance, but our attention is placed somewhere else. As I sit typing these words right now my eyes are focused on the computer screen but my attention (my external locus) in on the rooster I can see walking outside my window from the corner of my eye. While typing I can also place my external locus on the teacup on the table next to me. Neither the rooster nor the teacup is in visual focus but my attention, my "external locus" is placed squarely on them.

Our external locus is not necessarily constant; our attention can waver. And it will. When walking in the woods our attention will wander from the plants in our peripheral vision to the sensation of our feet on the ground to the sound of our breath to a telephone bill that we must pay next week. But that is the nature of our "monkey mind" and, as in any practice; it is our attention and intention that matter in the end. That is why they call it a "practice"; we must practice it before developing a level of skill. So we keep bringing our awareness back no matter how many times we waver. We will never get it "perfect", nor do we need to.

EXERCISE: External Locus Practice with Eye Focus

- Set a timer for one minute.
- Lengthen your spine; relax your eyes, jaw and face. Allow yourself to move into Stillpoint with your eyes open.
- Look at something and become completely absorbed by what you are seeing. Focus your attention on the minute details of what you are seeing. When the minute is up, close your eyes and try to see how much detail you can remember about what you saw.

External Locus Practice with Peripheral Vision

This exercise is a little more challenging: You are trying to observe details about something while not looking directly at it.

- Set a timer for one minute.
- Lengthen your spine; relax your eyes, jaw and face. Allow yourself to move into Stillpoint with your eyes open.
- Allow your eyes to rest gently on something with a soft focus. Select something else, out of the corner of your eye that you are going to pay attention to. Focus your attention on the minute details of what you observing out of the corner of your eye. When the minute is up, close your eyes and try to see how much detail you can remember about what you saw.

Advanced External Locus Practice with Peripheral Vision

This is an advanced practice and is the first step in reclaiming our Deep Listening skills.

- Set a timer for one minute.
- Lengthen your spine; relax your eyes, jaw and face. Allow yourself to move into Stillpoint with your eyes open.
- Allow your eyes to rest gently on something with a soft focus. Select something else, out of the corner of your eye that you are going to pay attention to. Focus your attention on how the object in your peripheral vision makes you *feel*. Notice what comes up in your body, no matter how weird or unrelated it may seem to be. When the minute is up, close your eyes and see if you can remember the feelings generated by the object in your peripheral vision.

EYE TRAINING
Do not stare at a disease. ~ Traditional Chinese medical proverb

Hakalau Eye Training
Hakalau or Owl Eyes is a non-linear type of vision, a "soft focus" with the eyes that includes a specific awareness of the peripheral vision. In Hakalau one is attentive to something without focusing on it visually.

In non-linear states of awareness the information we receive often comes in an indirect way. Sometimes it will appear to us as symbols within the mind's eye or as memories. It can also appear as emotions or as physical sensations.

Our peripheral vision consists of the outer limits of our field of vision, those movements and perceptions we perceive from the very fringes of our sight. Peripheral vision is very important when we are gathering plants. When we bring our attention to our peripheral vision, we encourage our unconscious mind to help us in absorbing information from our environment.

Hakalau eye training

Hakalau means "recipient of the leaf" or "opening to the leaf". Hakalau is a traditional Hawaiian practice that uses the peripheral vision to connect with the environment. When I use the term Hakalau in this book I am widening its' definition as a general term to include the practice of using the body, mind, and awareness to create sacred space around and within us. This sacred space is then used a platform from which to connect with our environment, but specifically to the plants in our environment.

In Hakalau we keep our attention on our peripheral vision while keeping our eyes on the distance in a soft focus. The head is set level but the eyes first look up and then slowly drop to a level direction first with the attention on the hands, and later on peripheral vision, on what is happening.

EXERCISE: Hakalau and Distal Focus
• Stand facing a plant or forest that is at least 20 feet away from you.
• Bring your hands together at arms length in front of your face, creating a triangle shape with your thumb and index fingers.
• Soft focus your eyes on something in the triangle created by your hands.

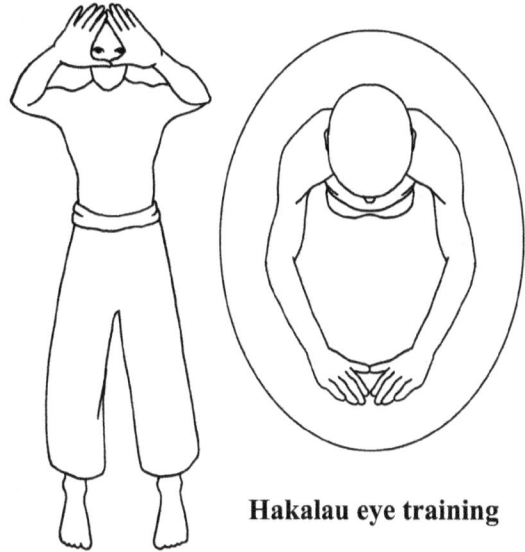

Visual Focus

External Locus on Hands

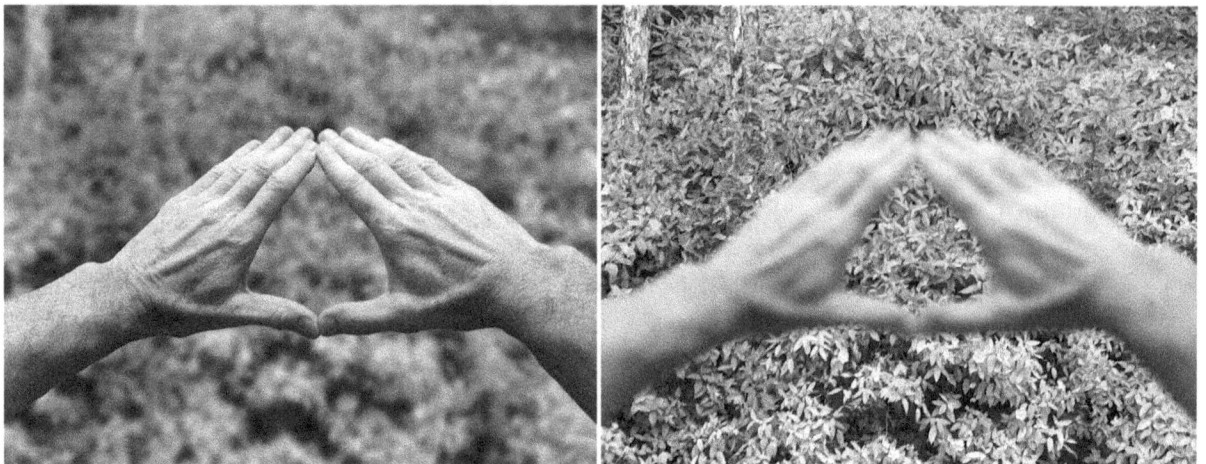

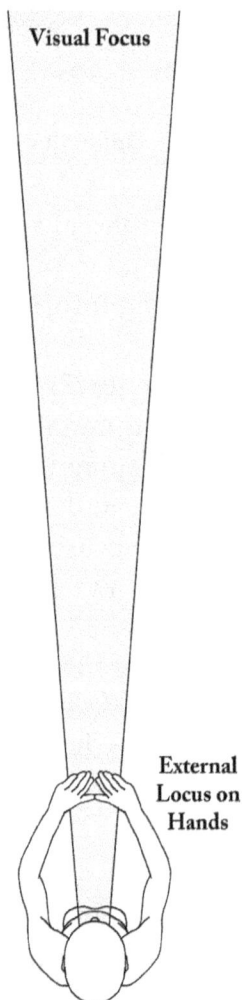

EXERCISE: Hakalau and External Locus

When you are comfortable with Hakalau and Distal Focus, try the following:

• Stand facing a plant or forest that is at least 20 feet away from you.

• Bring your hands together at arms length in front of your face, creating a triangle shape with your thumb and index fingers.

• Soft focus your eyes on something in the triangle created by your hands.

• Bring your external locus to your hands. What this means is that as your eyes are focused on the background, your attention, your external locus, is focused on your hands.

• While keeping your distal soft focus drop your hands keeping your external locus where your hands *were*. In other words, *your attention is brought to that which is not in visual focus*. This is the core practice of eye training. This shifts our awareness and, in doing so, our state of mind

Qigong Eye Training

In Qigong there is a practice where we bring our fingers in front of his eyes but we focus on something in the distance. As we look at something in the distance our awareness remains fixed on our fingers and the optical illusion of the orbs that are floating between them.

In Qigong the eyes are trained in a way very similar to Hakalau.

The hands are placed in front of the eyes, with fingers parallel. The eyes focus on the hands, which makes the background blurry. The eyes then focus on the background, which makes the hands blurry, but also creates an optical illusion of two orbs floating between the fingers.

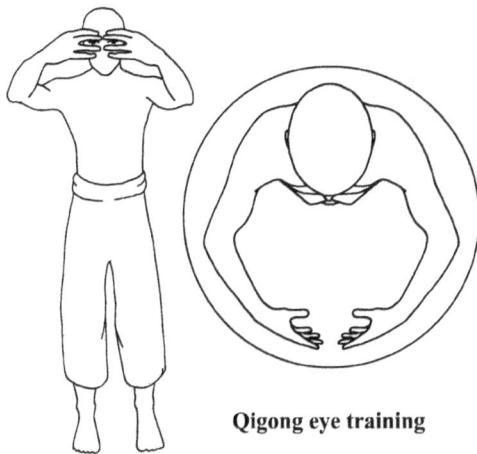

Qigong eye training

EXERCISE: Qigong and External Locus

• Stand you can see for more than 20 feet. You can either be outdoors or indoors looking out a window.

• Bring your hands about 16 inches in front of your face with fingers apart as in the image above. Your arms should be in a relative circle, as if you were embracing a large ball or a tree. Keep your shoulders relaxed and forward.

• Distal soft focus your eyes.

• While keeping your eyes distally focused, bring your external locus to the optical illusion of the orbs created by your fingers "overlapping".

• Drop your hands, keeping your soft focus on the background and your external locus where your hands just were.

Visual Focus

External Locus on peripheral vision

External Locus on peripheral vision

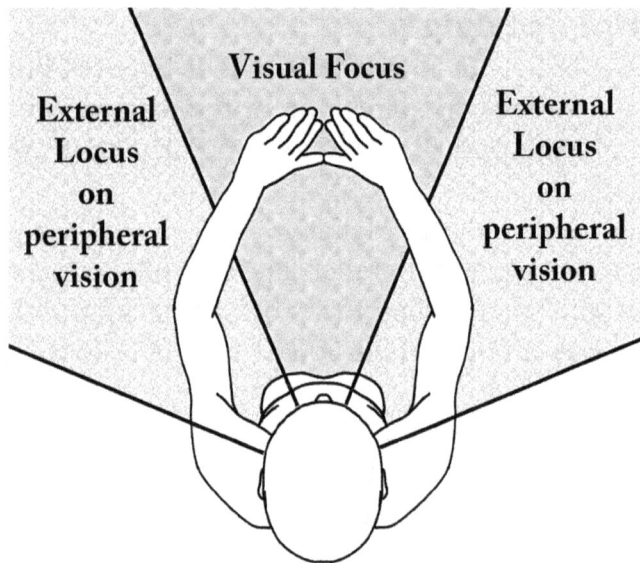

EXERCISE: External Locus on Peripheral Vision

Now we are ready to begin shifting our external locus to our peripheral vision.

This is a technique used in Deep Listening and plant gathering.

• Do either the Hakalau or the Qigong eye technique, bringing your external locus to your hands.

• Drop your hands, and when you are ready, shift your external locus from where your hands were to your peripheral vision on both sides.

EXERCISE: Shifting the External Locus Toward You

We will learn to shift back and forth from an internal locus to an external locus.

• Stand with your arms up in a Hakalau training stance.
• Soft focus your eyes on something in the distance.
• Bring your external locus to your hands, which are not in focus.
• Drop your hands and keep your external locus on the place where your hands just were.
• Bring your hands up in the same way, but this time make them 12 inches from your nose.
• Bring your external locus to your hands, keeping your visual soft focus on at a distance.
• Drop your hands and keep your external locus on the place where your hands just were.
• Repeat this, bringing your external locus closer and closer to your nose.

Shifting the External Locus to an Internal Locus

• Keep the soft focus of your eyes on the distance. After you have shifted your internal locus close to your nose, shift your external locus to an internal locus by bringing it inside your head.
• When this becomes comfortable, begin to drop your internal locus toward your na'au, your lower abdomen.
• Take note of any emotions or sensations this might bring up.

Naka

In Hawaiian language the word "naka" means to shake or quiver. When using Deep Listening skills in the forest special attention is paid to the way things move, particularly things in our peripheral vision.

Plants actually move a lot, but we seldom notice it. An obvious cause of movement is wind, but in traditional cultures, the way plants move is considered significant, a way to extract meaning and significance from the environment.

Does the wind actually speak to us? I don't know, perhaps. But I do know that if I approach a forest while keeping that open as a possibility, I become a more skilled and more observant practitioner. This is similar to how I feel about prayer: It's not our prayers that matter but who we become through praying.

EXERCISE: Naka

- Stand with your feet shoulder width apart, spine long, shoulders down and forward, eyes, jaw and muscles relaxed.
- Find a place to observe plants. A tree line at the edge of a meadow or road will work well.
- Bring your hands up and move into Hakalau, with your soft focus on the trees but your external locus on your peripheral vision.
- Drop your hands and pay close attention to any plant movement
- Clear your mind and awareness of anything except the movement that you are seeing. Imagine the movement as being one living, breathing organism.

EXERCISE: Naka / Hakalau / Dermis

- In the above exercise, try to feel the movement in your lower abdomen, your na'au. Notice if there are any differences in your bodily sensations as the movement of the plants changes.

Hakahele

Hakahele is Hakalau in motion, the practice of scanning the environment, especially in the forest, using peripheral vision and body sensitivity, while walking.

EXERCISE: Hakahele Practice

- Select a place in which you can walk comfortably where you will have a reasonably long line of site, such as a road or a flat path. If you need to wear a hat, choose one without a visor.
- Relax your body and begin walking. Select a pace from which you can gather information. It will probably be more slowly than your normal walking speed but does not have to be. Remember, you are not trying to "get" anywhere; you are gathering information from your environment.

- Select a spot on the horizon on which to focus your gaze as you walk toward it. Keep your eyes in soft focus.
- Choose something in your peripheral vision that you are going to track with your external locus. It should be roughly 20 to 40 feet ahead of you. It may be a cluster of leaves, a stone on the path, or a discoloration on a tree trunk.
- Keep your external locus on this object until it disappears completely from your field of view.
- Select another object on the opposite side as your external locus and track that.

EXERCISE: Advanced Hakahele Practice

- While moving in Hakahele, select two external loci, each 180° apart from each other. Track them simultaneously as they pass by. For example, one could be at 2 o'clock, and one could be a 7 o'clock.

- Select two different external loci, also 180° apart. One could be at 10 o'clock and one could be at 4 o'clock.
- Continue selecting diagonal patterns as you walk forward.

Breathing into the Heels

The men of old breathed clear down to their heels. - - Zhuang Zi, Nan Hua Jing

When we are in Hakalau (not moving) or Hakahele (moving) and we are breathing into our belly, most of our attention is involved in searching for movement and sensations through our peripheral vision and tracking the sensations in our abdomen, and on our skin. We may forget that there may be things going on behind us worthy of our attention.

When we breathe into our heels, we activate the meridians that run up the back of our body and over the top of our head. This allows us to more easily pay attention to what may be happening behind us.

There is another option open to us. We can breath into the Earth, or feel the Earth breathing into us. From this perspective our awareness can encompass both the "oval" shape defined by our front facing peripheral vision and an awareness to the rear. This can create a "sphere" of our awareness that encompasses all three dimensions.

EXERCISE: Earth Breathing Practice

- Stand with your feet shoulder width apart, spine long, shoulders down and forward, eyes, jaw and muscles relaxed.
- Your arms can be up as in the illustration or down at your sides.

Breathing into the Belly   **Breathing into the Heels**   **Breathing into the Earth**

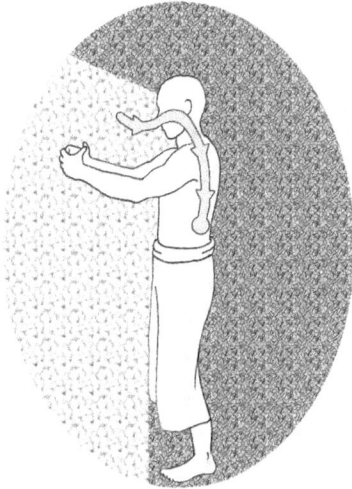

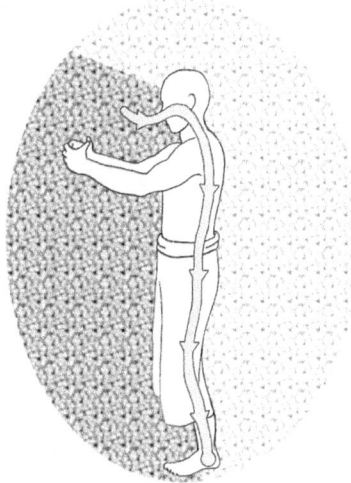

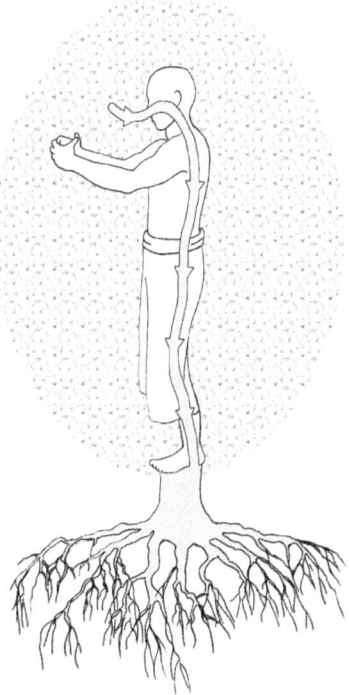

- Begin by relaxing your gaze and breathe into your belly. Allow yourself to be aware of what is happening in your field of vision, both where you are looking and in your peripheral vision.
- Now breathe deeper down your legs into your heels. Keep your eyes in soft focus. Notice that as you breathe deeper into your legs, your torso expands subtly to the rear. Try to feel temperature changes and other sensations from behind you.
- Finally, imagine yourself breathing deeply into the Earth. Allow a 360° orb to expand around you.

EXERCISE: Advanced Earth Breathing Practice

- As you breathe into the center of the Earth and feel all 360° around your body, shift your *internal locus* up and down your torso. Make note of any differences you experience with each change of position.

Labyrinth

Labyrinths have been used by numerous cultures all over the world to initiate and enhance non-ordinary states of consciousness. As far as I know they were not used in old Hawai'i. Ironically, one of the best ways I have found to learn the practice of Hakalau is in a labyrinth.

Walking a labyrinth can create a very similar state to that of Hakalau. I have some ideas as to why this may be so.

We enter a labyrinth with reverence, thereby creating sacred space. We quiet our minds and pay attention. This is exactly the same meditative state we create as we prepare to enter a forest to gather plants.

In a labyrinth we spend most of our time moving our bodies in a relaxed and with complete awareness. This also has a lot of similarities to the way we will move in a forest.

And lastly, when we are in a labyrinth there are often other people around us. We generally do not look directly at them when passing them in a labyrinth, but we are very conscious of their movements and we tend to track them out of the corners of our eyes. Tracking what passes by us using peripheral vision is exactly what is entailed in the practice of Hakalau and Hakahele.

If you can find a labyrinth nearby, you will find it a useful tool to enhance your Deep Listening skills. If you cannot locate one you can buy canvas labyrinths or instructions online for how to build your own. For more information you can go to www.HeartPath.com or purchase Eve Hogan's book *Way of the Winding Path: A Map for the Labyrinth of Life.*

EXERCISE: Labyrinth Practice

- It is impossible to get lost in a labyrinth and yet it's okay if you do. You can also lose your place occasionally; so if that happens, do not worry.
- Move at any speed you are comfortable. It is okay to pass others if they are going too slowly for you. Wait until you get near a 180° turn. When they are in the turn, step over the line and resume walking ahead of them.
- Before you enter a labyrinth, come into lucid waking, center yourself, and move into Stillpoint.

- When you are ready, enter they labyrinth. Keep your eyes in soft focus.
- Pay particular attention to your peripheral vision. If there are other people in the labyrinth notice what your body experiences as they walk by.
- Remember, ultimately there is no right or wrong way to walk a labyrinth.

Reading the Forest 'Backwards': Back Scanning

As Westerners, our eyes are strongly conditioned to move in very specific ways. Because we are trained from childhood to read from left to right our eyes move in predictable patterns. When we read we move our eyes relatively slowly from left-to-right, quickly zip them back from right to left. We then move on to the next line of text, repeating the pattern.

This pattern may serve us when reading text, but when we habitually default to

these "reading habits" in the forest, we can miss important details.

But we can take advantage of our conditioned eye movement patterns by disrupting them, allowing us to absorb more and unique information. We do this by reversing the by the way we scan with our eyes.

In much the same way that forgers bypass their personal writing habits by copying a signature upside down, or professional proofreaders read documents backwards to catch mistakes, we can trick our brain into picking up visual nuances.

EXERCISE: Back Scanning Practice

- Find a place in nature in which you are comfortable. Take the time to settle in to your body, moving into a state of relaxation.
- Allow your eyes to relax without losing the ability to keep a soft focus.
- Gently begin to scan slowly from right-to-left, return your gaze quickly to the right,

and scan again slowly from right to left. At first don't concern yourself with what you are seeing; spend time getting used to the sensation of moving your eyes this way.

- Always move your eyes more slowly toward the left and then more quickly toward the right
- Move from scanning things that are near to you to scanning things at a distance, and then coming back.
- When you become comfortable with this practice you can begin to do it while moving.

Preparing To Listen To Plants

Plants are all around us but very rarely do we pay attention to them. They create the air we breathe and the food we eat. Nothing in our life is possible without plants.

As a species we emerge from the same ecosystem as do plants, the same "ground of being". We are much closer to plants than we know. The material that creates nourishment in a plant, chlorophyll, is only one molecule different from material that transmits nourishment in our body, blood. Blood and chlorophyll are identical save that chlorophyll has magnesium at its core and blood carries iron.

We cannot *learn* to listen to plants. Listening to plants is not a skill that is learned, it is a skill that is *unlearned*. In order to hear what plants have to say to us we must unlearn our layers of conditioning that smothers our perceptions of the world. When we have sloughed off our layers, what is left is a kernel of our heritage as mammals. What remains is our possibility of connection with the rest of life. Small children listen to plants remarkably well, and they do so without training: They have less to unlearn.

As our species evolved and we became smarter and smarter monkeys, our intelligence came at a price. In order to acquire learned intelligence we had to sacrifice our instinctive intelligence. Not all of our instinctive intelligence was sacrificed, just enough to allow room for our new learned intelligence.

This is why native peoples always come back to the lower belly as a source of life and wisdom. Our learned intelligence is associated with our head. This is the neo-cortex that sits between our ears and gives us so much joy and anguish. But our more ancient and deeper intelligence is associated with the lower belly. Our lower belly is our connection to nature and to the natural world. It is the source of our "lost" intelligence, the intelligence of nature.

By bringing our attention back to this long forgotten part of our body and mind, we can reconnect with our instinctive intelligence. It is like a muscle, long dormant, that we can now begin to flex. As we use it, it will grow stronger with time.

If we do not recognize the possibility that plants may have something to tell to us, we will not listen to them in the first place. Once we are willing to accept that as a possibility, then we must practice listening. What we are practicing is the removal our mental cluter. In practicing we are again learning to trust that small faint voice inside us. At first that voice is barely audible, if we can hear it at all. But slowly, if we pay attention and are diligent, that voice will become stronger and clearer.

I consider listening to plants and gathering plants as separate and distinct activities. I may do one thing or the other, but generally I do not do both at the same time. When listening to a plant, the plant is the center of attention. When gathering plants for a patient, the patient is the center of attention. When you begin listening to plants I would not recommend doing anything else at the same time. In other words, set time aside to do just that.

However, when you are getting ready to listen to a plant, you may want to do a ritual *as if* you were going to gather plants. Creating a Kapu Space is a very useful ritual before spending time Deep Listening. It will help to put you in an appropriate frame of mind. In a sense, listening to a plant is a form of gathering, except that you are not gathering the plant itself, you are gathering information about the plant.

After you have done your ritual, you can move through the forest (or yard) and let your mind empty. Use a rooted gait and go into Hakahele (moving vision) and Hakalau (peripheral vision). Use your peripheral vision to shift into a more receptive mode. Allow yourself to relax and soak in what is around you. Feel the surrounding environment through your skin. Take your time. Notice changes in temperature and shifting sensations in your body.

Listening to Plants

Set aside at least an hour, preferably two. If you are like most of us it will take you at least that long to allow the mental chatter to subside a bit. Bring a cushion, blanket, or a chair with you unless you know that you will be sitting on comfortable grass or sand.

Turn your cell phone off. Do not write anything down while you are listening. Do not bring any books or writing material with you if you think you might be tempted to pick them up before you are done.

Select a plant that seems to be "calling" you, one for which you have an inexplicable affinity. Do not pull the plant out of the ground, or cut or tear leaves or branches; leave it in its natural state.

Sit down, make yourself comfortable, and mentally introduce yourself. Empty your mind. If you are sure that the plant is non-toxic, touch it and smell it. Pay particular attention to what happens in your body as you sit with this plant. What sensations are elicited? Where in your body do you feel them?

Notice what emotions, sensations, or images arise as you pay attention to this plant. *Do not edit yourself!* You may have thoughts of the president, or your grandmother, or a kitchen sink. You may feel anxious, bored, foolish, joyful, or annoyed. Your body may feel all manner of sensations: pain, discomfort, and tingling. You may feel nothing whatsoever. It does not matter. Just make a mental note of what is happening and go back to paying attention to the plant.

If I can do so comfortably, I will sometimes lay with my head resting on a part of the plant.

When you are done, thank the plant. Review what you have learned. See how much you can remember of your experience. If you want to you can then go back and write down your experience… or not. I use a "Rite in the Rain" book for my notes, a small field notebook with water resistant pages used by field biologists.

Once you have done this, you have made a friend. Your relationship to that plant will be changed forever.

Allow the information received to settle into your psyche over the following weeks and months. Some of it will make sense to you immediately, some will become apparent over time, and some of it will never make sense to you.

If you are 100% certain that the plant is not toxic and does not need special preparation, you can experiment with it a bit and see how it holds up to what you had experienced. Again, some things will fit, and some things will not.

Some plants will surprise you. When I first gathered *Eclipta alba* (han lian cao) in the wild, I discovered that the plant when used fresh causes stomach pain. The dried plant in the clinic has never done that.

Over time, as these plants become your friends, they will have more and more to say to you. And like some of our friends, they may self-disclose or not, depending on their mood and our ability to read nuances.

One day, you will notice that you are paying attention to your friends, loved ones, and patients in a different way. You find yourself viewing plants differently than you have before. Weeds are suddenly something interesting rather than a nuisance.

If you are a practitioner, you may find yourself using herbs in the clinic, differently. Ultimately, you may find yourself practicing a different kind of medicine. Rather than the medicine you have been taught, you may modify it so that now *all* of you is involved in the process, not just half of your brain.

EXERCISE: Listening to Plants

- Pick a place in nature that you can be comfortable. If you need to, bring a chair or a blanket with you so that you can be comfortable. Select a situation in which you will have minimal outside distractions. Turn off the ringer to your phone.
- Select a plant you wish to listen to. You may have decided which plant that is beforehand or you can choose one that you are attracted to for whatever reason.
- Ask permission to sit and listen to the plant. Wait for some kind of "response". It could be a confirmation such as a sudden breeze, the sound of a bird, or a sensation in your body.
- Spend an hour or two just sitting and listening to the plant. Use your body as an antenna. Make a mental note of any thoughts, emotions, or sensations that arise for you, but do not give in to the temptation to write anything down just yet.
- When you feel complete, thank the plant and write about your experience.

BRANCHES
Reaching Out - Listening to Each Other

BRANCHES
Reaching Out - Listening to Each Other

Qigong Breath with Partner

A lot of the rapport we share with others is based on an unconscious recognition of breathing patterns. It is not accident that the word "conspire" means "to breathe together". In both traditional Chinese and Hawaiian cultures breath is considered of primary importance to our physical, psychological, and spiritual health.

In the Chinese medical and spiritual arts, to practice Qigong is to work primarily with the breath, or "Qi". Qi also is a term that describes energy and life force. In Chinese medicine our personality and our character is sometimes described as our Qi.

The Hawaiian medical and spiritual arts the equivalent of Qigong is called Ho'omana. Ho'omana is the practice of building "Mana" or spiritual power. Some of the most potent Ho'omana practices are those that work with the Hä, or breath. In Hawaiian medicine our spiritual power and knowledge is sometimes described as our Hä.

EXERCISE: Partner Qigong - Mirror Breath

- Sit opposite your partner with your spine straight and your jaw relaxed.
- Relax your gaze on their face between their eyes.
- When you are ready, bring your breath into a pace that matches theirs.
- Make note of any sensations in your body as you do this.

Partner Qigong - Flow Breath

- Sit opposite your partner with your spine straight and your jaw relaxed.
- Relax your gaze on their face between their eyes.
- When you are ready, bring your breath into flow with theirs, that is, inhale when they exhale and exhale when they inhale.
- Make note of any sensations in your body as you do this.

Locus with a Partner

The place in our bodies that we identify as "ourselves" can influence our Deep Listening skills and the information we receive from our partner. In the following exercises pay attention to the subtle differences that emerge as you shift your internal locus.

EXERCISE: Internal Locus with a Partner - Breath

• Sit opposite your partner as you share a mirror breath.
• Relax your gaze on their face as they speak.
• When you are ready, bring your internal locus into your head. Notice what you are feeling in your body.
• Slowly drop your internal locus down to your throat, then chest, solar plexus and lower abdomen.
• With each shift in your internal locus, make note of any differing sensations for you as you gaze at your partner.
• Repeat the above process as you share flow breathing.

Internal Locus with a Partner - Listening

• Sit opposite your partner as they share something that is important to them.
• Relax your gaze on their face as they speak.
• When you are ready, bring your internal locus into your head. Notice what you are feeling in your body.
• Slowly drop your internal locus down to your throat, then chest, solar plexus and lower abdomen.
• With each shift in your internal locus, make note of any differing sensations for you as you listen to your partner.
• Discuss your observations then reverse roles.

Body As Antenna / Seeing with the Skin

Dermis Exercise with a partner: Sit or lie in a comfortable position and have your partner move their hands over the surface of your body without actually touching you. Notice the sensations of warmth from their hands. Do different areas of your body respond differently to the sensations created by their hands?

Naka

Our relationship to naka, quivering or shaking, is different in a partner than it would be if we were listening to the forest. In the context of our relationship our, naka is a reference to incongruent or revealing body language.

Poker players use a similar concept to determine if their opponent is bluffing. In that situation it is referred to as a "tell": a physical manifestation of psychological stress.

But we are not using this concept to determine our partner's honesty. We are using it to help us understand them better. In our partnership, a naka could be any incongruent or revealing body language, but for our purposes we are going to focus on the naka that is revealed around the eyes

EXERCISE: Naka Partner Exercise

In this exercise we place our external locus strongly on the eyes of our partner.

- Sit opposite your partner and come to a state of lucid waking.
- You and your partner will have a conversation, but one of you will primarily be speaking (the "speaker") and the other will be primarily observing (the "listener").
- The speaker should talk about something that is going on in their life.
- The listener may ask questions but they should their attention and external locus on the speaker's face and eyes.
- When the speaker references something that touches on their personal shadow, there will be a brief flicker of facial tension, usually around the eyes. This may be very fast, lasting only a microsecond. This flicker of incongruence, of facial tension, is a quiver, or a Naka.
- The listener should take note of the subjects or people that elicit a naka in the speaker. The listener then asks a question about the subject that triggered the naka. If the subject again triggers a naka, that implies that the topic involves a piece of shadow for the speaker.
- This information can help both the speaker and the listener. It benefits the speaker in that it can make them conscious of unconscious currents running through their psyche. It benefits the listener in that they have more information about the speakers shadow and can make choices around how they choose to navigate it.

Reading Strangers

It is very useful to take quick energetic "snapshots" of people in public places. We process huge amounts of information about people every day but the processing is preconscious; it normally occurs beyond our level of awareness. When we read strangers we make our unconscious process more lucid. When we read strangers as an exercise it not only shows us the shadows of our biases, but also reveals how much we arc already using our Deep Listening skills in everyday life.

EXERCISE: Reading Strangers

- Go to a public place such as an airport, shopping mall, or any busy sidewalk.
- Airports are better for learning to consciously recognize body language because travelers often have stronger emotions than shoppers. People in airports often very sad or angry, and usually very stressed. Shopping malls are better for reading people's energetic nuances. Stress levels are lower shopping malls and people tend to be somewhat less guarded.
- As you walk by people, notice what thoughts come into your mind about them and what physical sensations accompany your thoughts.
- Don't worry about being too "judgmental". You may be correct or incorrect in your

assessment, but that does not matter. The point is to learn to tune in to your physical body and your perceptions.

- Your "snapshot" may be something like "Had too much to drink", "Embarrassed to be seen with their companion", "Having a great day", "Cheapskate", "Dangerous", "Easy to get along with", etcetera.

- Realize that your observations may be accurate… or not. If you end up meeting the person you observed, don't base your interaction with that person on your snapshot, but definitely file the observation away for future reference.

- If you can figure out specifically which cues and biases are feeding you the information on which you base your snapshots, that is fine. But don't spend too much time trying to rationally dissect your observations. The point of this exercise is to develop conscious use of your Deep Listening skills.

David Bruce Leonard

LEAVES & FLOWERS
A Gathering of Friends

LEAVES & FLOWERS
A Gathering of Friends

ACTIVATING THE CONNECTION: UNDERSTANDING OUR FRIENDS
Why Gather Medicines?

Another definition of medicine might be: Anything that contributes to the integration of the individual within themselves and the integration of that person with the natural world. Plants can be an important part of that contribution.

As practitioners we are cogs in a vast machine; one that is, in many ways, too immense to fathom. Still, the universe gives us hints, subtle and obtuse, that point us in the direction we need to look.

This is why gathering medicines can help anyone who practices any kind of medicine. Even a surgeon or a psychiatrist would find the practice of gathering medicines help her connect to her patients, or at the very least, she might uncover something about herself in the process ….

Gathering medicines can re-connect us to the natural world, and to the field from which that integration emerges, Gathering medicines strongly connects us to both the inspiration and source of our tools. This attunement to natural processes has always been part and parcel of indigenous medicines and our quality of life as a whole.

At first this attunement leads us to other medicines. Ultimately, if we are diligent and sincere, it leads the medicines to gather us.

What I am sharing is an aggregation of information drawn from different traditions and practices. This is eclectic and has been pared down as to what has worked for me. I encourage you to take from this what works for you and to leave the rest behind.

Preparing to Gather
OVERVIEW OF PLANT GATHERING

- The knees are bent and the center of gravity is low. The gait is comfortable.
- Feel the environment with your skin.
- Breathe into and from the earth.
- Lumbar and cervical curves are flattened.
- Consecration is done with the breath from the nose.
- Visual awareness is in the peripheral vision.
- Proprioceptive/somatic awareness in close to or within the body. It goes from distant, to near the head, to inside the head, and into the belly. This is 360° awareness.
- Left hand for a woman, right hand for a man.
- West side for a woman, east side for a man.
- Gather going downhill.
- Watch for and pay attention to signs or omens (hö'ailona), and their meaning (hö'ike).
- Gather early in the day

If gathering in the early morning in the dark (as did some of my Hawaiian teachers) it is important that you have scoped out the area in which you will travel. It is also important to let someone know where you will be going should you not return by a certain time.

A Plant Gathering Protocol

1. Ho'omalu - Centering and Ho'omahalo - Gratitude

Centering is the process of aligning ourselves with the outside world while stabilizing our interior terrain. Gratitude, as my Hawaiian teachers always said, is one emotion that will never betray us.

2. He Makana - A Gift

Because when we visit a forest we are visiting our elders and ancestors, we always have something to offer them to show our respect and appreciation. Traditionally, the best gift one could leave was ones voice, ka 'ölelo, in the form of a chant. But anything from a song played on a flute, to a prayer, to beautiful thoughts and appreciations will do.

3. 'Ae- Permission - May I gather from this place?

We ask permission to show respect and to check to make sure that the inner and outer worlds are aligned with our intentions in gathering medicines for our patients.

4. *Introduction - Announcing yourself to the forest*
We introduce ourselves to the elders who make up this forest.

5. *Genealogy - Where am I from?*
In Polynesian societies, genealogy was all-important. It defined your status, your activities, the person you married, your profession, and your relationship to the Gods and to the world.

In canoe cultures where conflict was frequent, people would attempt to ascertain familial relationships when meeting strangers. Long ago, one's genealogy was tattooed on one's body as a source of pride, but also in order to align with one's ancestry.

Because the plants in a forest are considered ancient beings, when we give our genealogy we are introducing ourselves and determining any familial relationships.

6. *Who am I gathering for?*
The person for whom you are gathering medicines is named.

7. *Why am I gathering, to what end?*

Your specific reasons for gathering for this patient are named. This is done so that you will have clarity as to the outcome you are seeking. For example, if a patient were to have a skin condition, you would name the patient, identify the specific issue the patient was having, and try to find the specific plant or combination of plants that would realign that patient with their health, their family, their kuleana (duty) and their integrity.

8. *Mihi - Why am I really here?*
When we "mihi", we become accountable and take responsibility for all of how we show up. "Shadow" is a term that refers to the parts of ourselves that we hide, repress, or avoid. In this protocol, we search for a part of ourselves that might have an ulterior motive. We might be gathering herbs because we had to get away from the kids, because we need the money, or because we are avoiding something else that we need to do. So, we take a look at our "shadow", and in doing so we shine a light of compassion and acceptance on those parts of ourselves that may need healing. We offer up the less desirable parts of ourselves to the forest, and in doing so, become the kind of practitioner we would like to be.

9. Giving thanks. Again, Gratitude.

So, a typical protocol may be done out loud or silently and might go something like this:

Meditation, Prayer, or Chant.

Recognition of Ke Kuahiwi (the mountain), Ka ʻÄina (the land), and Ke Kai (the ocean) as the source of who we are and from which we receive blessings.

A gift is then given to the forest.

May I gather plants from this forest? I am David Bruce Leonard, a student of Hawaiian medicine under Kahu Kawika Kaʻalakea. I am descended from the Northern European families of Leonard, Lincoln, Rich, Heyndrickx, and DeNutte. I am here gathering for my patient XXXX so that she can heal the sores on her legs and stabilize her blood sugar. (The patient is visualized throughout this process as having healthy legs, mobility, and vitality). *I am here also because I needed to get out of the house.*
Thank you. I vow to honor, sustain, and nourish this Wao Akua as my kuleana (privilege / responsibility).

This flexible protocol can be used in many situations and the steps can become unconscious habits. The subject of traditional gathering methods can be very complex. Again if you are interested in gathering herbs, you should receive instruction from a traditional practitioner.
My Hawaiian teachers always said that there is no medicine in the plants; the true medicine is our relationship to God.

Consecrating with the Hä

When we wish to set an intention with a plant (or a patient) we use the breath as a consecration. When we do this we visualize our intention as we exhale through the nose onto the plant.

HEAVEN - YANG
Conclusions

HEAVEN Yang
Conclusions

'Ōhāhā ka hua kūpuna -- The fruit of our elders thrive.
- - traditional Hawaiian saying

The Earth is our witness. She is our Mother.
We embrace our shadow and our light, our Earth and Heaven.
We have nothing to prove; we accept who we are.
We carry forth the traditions and lessons of those who have come before.
We ask for their help in bringing our Blessed Home back into balance.